DO I MAKE SENSE?

FAHIMA NIAZ

Copyright © Fahima Niaz
All Rights Reserved.

This book has been published with all efforts taken to make the material error-free after the consent of the author. However, the author and the publisher do not assume and hereby disclaim any liability to any party for any loss, damage, or disruption caused by errors or omissions, whether such errors or omissions result from negligence, accident, or any other cause.

While every effort has been made to avoid any mistake or omission, this publication is being sold on the condition and understanding that neither the author nor the publishers or printers would be liable in any manner to any person by reason of any mistake or omission in this publication or for any action taken or omitted to be taken or advice rendered or accepted on the basis of this work. For any defect in printing or binding the publishers will be liable only to replace the defective copy by another copy of this work then available.

To Hafsah

Contents

1. twenty

At thirteen years old, I started writing
Broken rhyme schemes of thoughts that crossed my mind
grammatically incorrect sentences
most of which barely made any sense
At fourteen, I wrote what people asked of me
I wrote about issues that were not my own.
I wrote about a world not my own
I didn't write for myself
But I let everything not my own fill the void of my sanity
At fifteen, I almost gave up writing
I picked up a brush instead, in hopes of expressing more
It helped
but a part of me still woke up with verses to keep
At sixteen, I let all hell loose
I wrote about every little reflection
I wrote about the stars, the moon, and the sky—how it held
together all of its vastness
At seventeen, I started to make more sense
I pictured my feelings and put them into art
I poured my soul into anything blank
I spilled the contents of my mind and felt lighter but never
empty
At eighteen, I became more confident

I started to write every single one of my words with so much
assertion that it almost burned through the pages
I was stubborn and built up rage that could only be written
away
At nineteen, my heart grew fonder of my younger self
I wrote day and night
I wrote about ghosts and put myself in the shoes of other
people
I wrote about nostalgia and how my heart was a burial ground
At twenty now
I'm writing about half-truths and other ridiculous things like
love.
Ripping pieces of myself apart and calling it art

2. empathy

When I look into the mirror,
I see a girl struggling.
Unsure and tired,
She doesn't seem to realise
how much she matters.
To the people around her
A mother would look at the girl.
and see a smile.
That could mend a thousand stitches.
A sister would see
Happiness and comfort
In the girl I'm looking at
A friend will find a ray of light.
In the individual that they
trust with their entire lives.
I don't see that person.
But I have to understand
To exist is to be.
seen from others' perspective
Maybe one day.
If she could, this girl would be nicer to herself.
Maybe one day.
I will show empathy toward myself.

3. forgotten

I had a poem stuck in my head.
It had been humming in the background.
A few days ago, it started screaming its presence.
I tried to recall it.
But all it left was a murmur.
Every time I write, I am reminded
of the words that never came out.
Words that are forgotten
I fill those empty spaces.
With an aftertaste of remembrance,
When something is perfect, you can tell.
It lingers longer than it lasts.
My words have so much emotion.
But none of it is ever quite true.
They're versions of what was felt.
Not by me, perhaps, but somewhere

4. rebuilding

You heard something shattering miles away.
shattering into many little pieces.
On the floor, it was a mess.
I stood there pale, dull, and numb.
You realised what had broken.
There was no delicate glass.
But pieces of what remained of me
You wanted to pick up the pieces.
You wouldn't stop.
No matter how much I tried to
You bent down and touched a sliver.
Immediately, your hands were bleeding.
Crimson-red hands patching up wounds
I did warn you before.
Fixing what's broken sometimes
It ends up causing new scars.
red, shattered, and scattered.
Two broken people stood there.
Rebuilding each other

5. exhausted

Aren't we all just waiting to be told?
that we are understood.
and that we are
Neither too much nor too little.
We are not being dramatic.
and crying for no reason.
It does not need to be explained all the time.
Aren't we all a little exhausted?
Not having to explain ourselves
I had to question it after.
I must have said something stupid.
And then regret.
Does it get tiring at times?
What makes more sense now is
My mind works
By fixating on things
all at once.
all too much
or nothing at all.
There is no in-between.
There are no better things.
There is no silence or peace.
There is too little to hold on to.

Or too much to let go.

What I am trying to tell you

is that I don't have a middle ground.

I am not still and quiet.

Or loud and exhausting.

All I am doing is wavering.

from place to place.

6. a story

There are times when I have a story to tell

A story to practically yell out loud

A story with no end yet might be tragic

This story is not long or full

It's not a novel that will make you sob

I will tell you all the pieces

Every plot point has intricate details

very mundane that at one point you wouldn't even remember

You wouldn't remember

All the things I told you

About this story

The girl and her unkempt existence

You will not be thrilled to listen

I know you probably don't even want to listen

But this story might just make more sense

If only you listened

Careful I do dramatise things here and there

But will you still listen?

If I told you all I ever did was mope around sunsets

And don't actually have it that bad

I spilled all my secrets and yet there might never be a plot twist

This story, as I said, is one without an ending

And just like this poem
This story contains no visible pattern
It's about this girl stuck in daydreams
It repeats several times
Would you still listen to me?
Do you still want to listen?

7. no name

Tragedies have names, and so do mine

It flattered with greatness and flunked just like a moth

Questions are important and the answers are not very much

There is this imminent landscape of words in me that no one will want to listen to. Not a soul, not a feather, not a living fable would do.

The paper caught on fire for pointing out this disappointment that held the pen.

Agony and filtered agony would fester in self-hate. Let me destroy it then

Let me destroy things Let me take the blame, for that is the one thing I can do effortlessly.

Let me be the one to die on this battlefield, for I'd rather die than be called a candle in the wind.

I don't want to be the woman who handles your wounds and caresses your soul

I'll cease to exist the moment you call me mad

This is what I do

This is who I am: a mad woman who was disregarded

A mad woman who had an ocean of emotions inside of her

Does something inside you burn?

I think I have my ashes, but they're not all mine.

8. will you?

There are words I cannot write
Not because I don't know how to
I know exactly how to form the sentences
I know exactly what will make my eyes bleed
All the perfect lies
That will rip me apart
I don't write them, because I am afraid
I'm afraid of letting it out
Would I feel empty with what haunts me
Or would it haunt me anyway?

9. i have it all together

I have it all together.
I tell myself I have it all together.
all my worries and all my dreams.
I have it all laid out.
I have a list of things I want.
and a list of realistic thoughts.
I do not rely on my dreams.
When I know how I'll end up
It keeps killing me.
But I have it all together.
People really care about me.
And I have the freedom
I can cry whenever I want.
I know it sounds good.
And it is indeed good.
I know my thoughts.
My contained reality is ideal.
In a way, I am lucky, perhaps.
But yet I keep telling myself
I have it all together.
Because what else could I want?
From this life:
From this beautiful tragedy:

I am convinced.

If I keep telling myself

Whispering constantly

That I will someday

Have it all together

10. art

I have realised this over the past months

I allow myself to write when I feel like a total disaster

I allow myself to pour out words when there's nothing else I can do

Which is to say, I write my sorrows

Everything I put down makes so much sense

When my mind is a total mess

And maybe I will remain in this state of vulnerability

just to save my poetry

It does seem a little pathetic

You must be thinking

That I am crazy for wanting to be in this state

If it helps, let me tell you

I tried writing when I was happy

It didn't make me feel anything

It was good, but never enough

I was good but never extraordinary

The question was now:

Do I destroy myself to be acknowledged?

Should I break apart?

And then I call my broken pieces art.

11. reassurance

I need to understand the difference between
Being tolerated and knowing when I am needed
Sometimes I hate the way my mind works
It needs reassurance every once in a while
I jump into waves no matter how deep or shallow they look,
as long as they seem to look like they'll give me what I need
To be understood is reassuring
Confidence is reassuring
Being treated as if I am required is reassuring
Not when I start to idealise all these thoughts
without any of them being communicated to me
I don't know if you've read this far
But if you have
I want to reassure you
I am proud of you.
Please breathe
and understand that you are required
You add so much to the lives of people around you.

12. see

You see, a sinking ship is in the distance
The majority of it was rusted and struggling
Its dim light gets lost on the horizon
The sun hasn't risen and in perfect silence,
You see it still as the waves wreak worry
There are shivers down your spine
You see what's sinking?
But it's beautiful even in misery
It's dying like it needs to.
You know exactly the destruction you witness
You know the despair you see
All too familiar, all just a memory.
You want to help, but the water is cold
When you jump, you will drown too
So you just watch and that's it
The sun rises and that's it
There's nothing on the waves
Perhaps you could have done something
But everything feels warm and you're already tired
Close your eyes; there's nothing left to see.

13. i know a man

I know a man who's almost there
in his mind and snare
a touch childish and grey
I know a man who's not morally wrong
Who knows what to say
And maybe he might not run away
I know a man who, dare I say,
might not even be the same
a void with the soul intact
I know a man who's paranoid
But would still call me insane
I know a man who cares enough
But would still let me walk away
I know a man who's loud enough
But what's louder would be his emptiness
Unabashedly, being alive
This man will cry if you let him
Maybe he's been neglected
I know a man who's bruised
He has stitches that won't show
I know a man so cheerful
His sorrow would look yellow
I know a man I think

He'd never let me know
What he is or was
I am afraid I never knew this man

14. until i can't

I do not know what I should write about anymore

The grey sky or the fact that I miss the girl I was when I was ten

I want to be able to not hesitate

To not bother if my art looks appealing

To not bother if my words cut you like a knife

I want to smile and not have anything to define it

I want to be a better person than I am

But the fact that my younger self would be proud of me

Is what makes me not stop

So I will write words that don't make sense

I will write sentences and paragraphs about anything and everything

I will write about your problems

Until I get the courage to write about mine

I want to make art that people cannot look away from

I want to not be frightened about losing myself

Because who am I if I am unable to?

Let myself be known

Let myself be heard

I will do all these things

Until I know I can't

15. i cannot

There are times I want to write about,
how I picture a person
And I stop myself from doing so.
I stop myself before my words settle in.
Do you understand that it's not just a few words put together?
But I'm pouring my heart into them
I don't want to pour out my heart
into the idea of someone
If my words get lost in an ocean of thoughts,
I would rather never write about you
for the fear of not being able to stop
for the fear of knowing all these words by heart
Being afraid helped me stay sane.
I was so afraid I didn't write about you
Instead, I wrote about how I could not.

16. nostalgia

nostalgia is just an obscure emotion

what am I reminiscing about?

the fatality of the brutal sky each day

Do I remember the countless stars?

That I didn't notice once or twice

It's the fact that there was something that felt

And whatever remained turned blue

You're telling me that I have to be saddened

I have to go through a memory lane

Each and every time something small is mentioned,

That peculiar smell can make me cry

No, the child I was did not make all this up

The faults of my marginal mind

Facing the consequences of nostalgia

It's like an everlasting burn

That does not fade away

but it always feels like it's fading

Vivid memories have new faults every time

This longing is a burden

A sad, tragic reminder that I survived

17. face

When I was younger,
I hated looking at the mirror
It was a subconscious habit
I would not bother to realise
That I looked like this
to recognise my face
To observe it and remember it
It was like I was avoiding myself
I was avoiding finding a word
To describe the way I looked
This became clear to me much later.
that it wasn't the best thing
I should stare at myself
Look at me and acknowledge me.
Look at the spots and scars
Understand my characteristics.
know this face
Remember all of it

18. distraction

My hands were stained with black ink from the paper I had been holding

a pause in which my mind wandered to worrying and then counting the pages

easily distracted, and now a little burnt out

Every sign of anxiety was being ignored

I shred paper that had the wrong sentences and threw them out

I am thinking and setting out a scene in my head

I had two podcasts paused on two different screens in front of me

scattered words and a clock ticking in the background

Slowly, the weight of my head regained more attention

Ignoring it again This time I was distracted by something else

The ticking in the background wouldn't let me do anything else.

and it breaks my mind-every little sound

Yet the ticking was the loudest

distracted again, this time by the noise outside

It was off-putting that people made a lot of noise when you noticed them

There was ringing going on on some screen

And my toes were shaking now that I started to notice; it wouldn't stop
I am distracting myself from all this by breathing a little loud
I found it difficult if I focused on it
What do I distract myself with this time?

19. loneliness

A movie I didn't watch is paused.
melted candles that lost their scents
When evening came, the fire was still burning.
I clean my brushes until my hands are wrinkled
Then shut the windows and close all the doors
The cats in the neighbours' house are shrieking
The kitchen light is flickering
No sound comes out of this household
plates clattering and not a single one used
There's food in pots and there's water leaking somewhere
What picture is painted in your mind?
Is it loneliness or just a cosy little home?
Is it loneliness or just some girl living her dream?
Is it loneliness or are you afraid?

20. why i write

I am writing today because the women in my family are vicarious speakers
They speak every word with the utmost confidence
They tell me stories of how they lived and how I should too
They tell me fear is only momentary
They hold the hilt of an invisible sword
Sharpened edges and sharper remarks
They walk with their heads held high and tell me that it's okay to cry
I am in awe of them and will never stop talking about them.
They love everything that they have
They're all artists, all of them in their own way
I admire them
I know I can never be as strong
They teach me so many things
The women in my family are like pillars
Their words are louder than mine
They speak English with so much grace you question your own tongue
I strive to be the burning light they portray into existence each day
They tell me that I shouldn't set myself back
The women of my family are fighters and combatants

They plunge into war and always know exactly what to do

I am not as confident or as audacious

But I know that I'll do something right

because the women in my family tell me that I am doing just

fine

I am emotional and exactly as they are

I am stubborn and make decisions quickly

They always stand apart, and maybe I carry some of that with

me

I am unpredictable and scared of responsibility

I am not everything I can be, but I know where to start

The women of my family are the reason I don't hold back

The generations of their voices

They have made me exactly the way I am

So now, whenever I speak, write, or express myself,

I will continue to echo each of their lives

www.ingramcontent.com/pod-product-compliance
Lightning Source LLC
Chambersburg PA
CBHW051335160726
47995CB00004B/1099